FOCUS ON

EARLY PEOPLE

MICHAEL BENTON

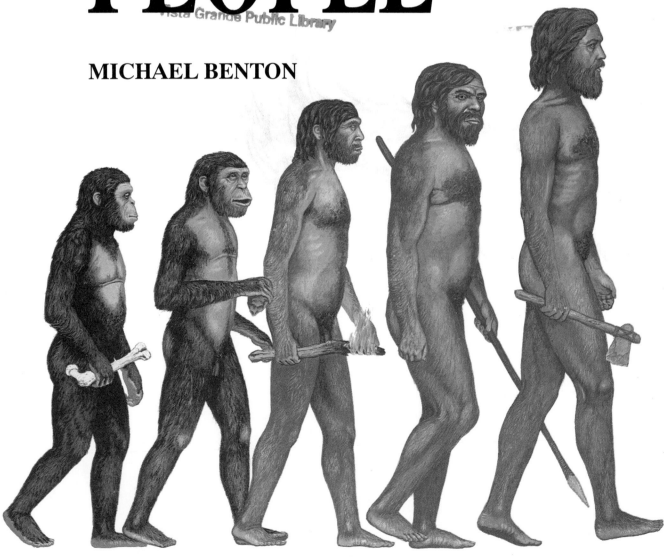

SHOOTING STAR PRESS

This edition produced in **1995** for
Shooting Star Press Inc
Suite 1212, 230 Fifth Avenue
New York, NY 10001

© Aladdin Books Ltd 1995

Created and produced by
Aladdin Books Ltd
28 Percy Street
London, W1P 9FF

*First published in
the United States in 1995 by*
Shooting Star Press

ISBN 1-57335-156-3

Design	David West Children's Book Design
Designer	Edward Simkins
Series Director	Bibby Whittaker
Editors	Susannah Le Besque
	Angela Travis
Picture research	Brooks Krikler
	Picture Research
Illustrators	David Burroughs
	James McDonald
	James Field
	Alison Brown

The author, Michael Benton PhD., is a Reader in the Department of Geology at Bristol University. He has written many books and papers on early people and prehistoric life, and is involved in researching the field of prehistory.

INTRODUCTION

The search for our origins is probably as old as humanity itself. But it has only been with the birth of modern science that the story of human origins has become clearer. Some discoveries have been difficult for people to accept because they contradicted beliefs that have been held for centuries. Scientists have pieced together fragments of information to build up a picture of what early people looked like, how they walked, what they ate and how they communicated. However, there are still huge gaps in our knowledge which scientists can only fill with guess work. This book tells the story as we know it so far.

Geography
The symbol of planet Earth shows where geographical facts are included. These sections include a look at how early people migrated across the world and at the impact of climatic change on human evolution.

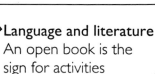

Language and literature
An open book is the sign for activities which involve language and literature. These sections examine the development of speech in humans and take a look at the character of Tarzan the ape man.

Science
The microscope symbol indicates where science information is included. These sections look at how scientists reconstruct an entire skeleton  from only a few pieces of bone, and how the diseases early people suffered from can be detected by examining bones.

History
The sign of the scroll and hourglass shows where historical information is given. These sections look at key people involved in the discovery of important fossils, and at the famous Piltdown fake.

Social history
The symbol of the family indicates where information about social history is given. These sections include a look at how early people made fire and how they hunted and cooked meat.

Arts, crafts and music
The symbol showing a sheet of music and art tools signals arts, crafts or musical activities. Topics covered include a look at the cave paintings left by Cro-Magnon peoples and the portrayal of early people in movies.

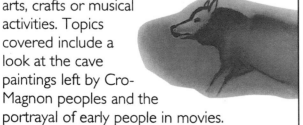

CONTENTS

THE FIRST PRIMATES

Humans, monkeys and apes belong to a group of mammals called primates. The first primates appeared in the Northern Hemisphere about 70 million years ago. They were tree-dwelling squirrellike animals that bore little resemblance to modern primate species. It took another 30 million years before the first monkeys and apes evolved. Today there are more than 180 primate species.

Film fantasy
Authors and film makers have always been fascinated by the mystery of our origins. The hugely successful film *2001, A Space Odyssey*, made in 1968, is based on a short story by Arthur C. Clark. This science fiction fantasy, explores the question of what triggered humans to make tools and thus set us apart from other animals. The scene from the film (below) shows the first human ancestor to use a bone as a tool.

Early mammals
The first mammals (above) evolved about 210 million years ago, at the time of the very first dinosaurs. They probably lived alone and were nocturnal (active at night). These early mammals are called 'archaic' mammals because they are the distant relatives of living animals rather than direct ancestors.

The march through time
The first monkeys evolved 40 million years ago, and the first apes 30 million years ago. Apes and humans probably shared a common ancestor until between 10 and 6 million years ago when the line of evolution to humans and apes separated.

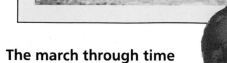

First monkeys
40 million years ago

First apes
30 million years ago

Brain development

The gradual increase in brain size is one of the most notable characteristics of human evolution. *Australopithecus* had a brain about one third the size of a modern human brain. The brains of *Homo habilis* and *Homo erectus* got larger through time; as their brains developed, so did their ability to make tools, use fire and hunt.

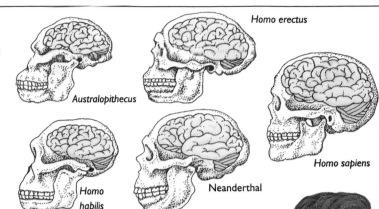

Australopithecus

Homo erectus

Homo habilis

Neanderthal

Homo sapiens

Australopithecus, lived between 5 and 1 million years ago. They were small upright walkers with ape-sized brains. The species *Homo* came into being about 2 million years ago, evolving into *Homo sapiens* (modern humans) about 35,000 years ago.

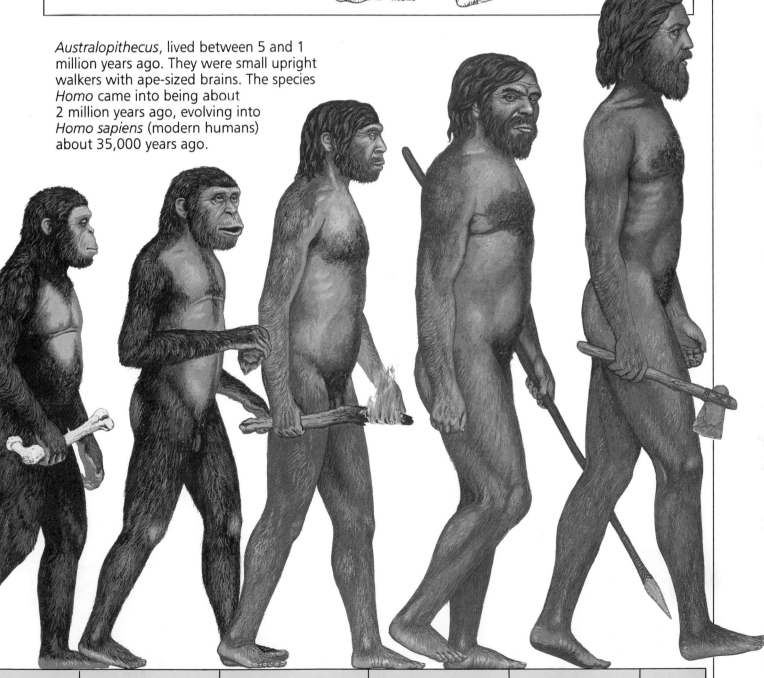

Australopithecus	Homo habilis	Homo erectus	Homo neanderthalensis	Homo sapiens
5-2 million years ago	2-1.5 million years ago	1.5 million - 500,00 years ago	500,000-35,000 years ago	35,000 years ago

OUR PRIMATE RELATIVES

Modern non-human primates have large and intricate brains; they are more intelligent than other land mammals. Although most primates live in trees, apes and monkeys are like humans in many other ways: they have forward facing eyes and some are omnivorous – they eat both plants and meat. Most primates look after their young for a long time, and teach them all the skills necessary for living a complex life.

Communication

The similarity between apes and humans is quite obvious and has led scientists to observe apes in order to learn more about the human race. There has been some debate as to whether chimps can be taught to communicate as humans do. Efforts to teach chimps to speak failed because of their vocal cord design. Some chimps have been taught to use sign language, but it is difficult to know whether they use it in the same way we do. Some scientists claim that chimps are able to use sign language to make observations as well as to communicate basic needs.

Humans and chimps can form close attachments.

Chimpanzees

There are two chimp species, the common and the pygmy. They are equally happy in the trees and on the ground, and live in family groups.

Gorillas

Gorillas spend most of their time on the ground. They walk on all fours, using the knuckles of the hands as well as the soles of the feet.

Diet

Primates eat a wide range of food. Gorillas are vegetarian and chimps eat mainly fruit, though they have been seen killing and eating small monkeys. Most vegetarian primates have adapted to either a leaf or a fruit and nut-based diet, because the teeth and stomach have to be different to digest each food type.

Monkeys

There are two main groups of monkeys, the South American monkeys which have long tails that can grasp branches like a fifth leg, and the Old World monkeys of Africa and Asia, which either have non-grasping or very small tails.

Orangutan

The orangutan of Southeast Asia is a tree-climber. It uses its arms and legs to swing among the branches. Orangutans are fruit eaters.

Ape skeleton

All the bones in an ape skeleton (right) can be matched with human bones, but there are distinct differences. Apes are not designed to stand upright for long because the hip bones and backbone slope forwards. Their arms are usually longer than their legs because they use them to swing through the trees, and their skull is smaller. However, like humans, apes have no tail.

Tarzan

The American author, Edgar Rice Burroughs created the character of Tarzan in the 1900s. Tarzan was the son of a Scottish nobleman who was lost in the African jungle as a child and was cared for by the apes. Tarzan is famous for swinging through the trees uttering a strange cry and beating his chest. Tarzan has featured in many popular films.

WHAT ARE OUR ORIGINS?

For thousands of years humankind has been preoccupied by the question of its origins. Many cultures have legends explaining how and why humans were created. In the last 200 years these have given way to scientific explanations. Evidence from fossils has convinced most scientists that human beings developed over millions of years. However, we still do not know the whole story, and there are many unanswered questions about the exact pattern of human evolution.

Digging up the bones

Early human fossils are found buried in the ground. Scientists use picks, trowels and brushes (left) to dig carefully around artefacts on the dig site. The smallest fragments may be very important. The dig site (right) is carefully mapped so that every find can be located. Dozens of people are often needed for the slow, careful work.

Charles Darwin

Charles Darwin (1809-1882) was one of the first scientists to suggest that humans were closely related to apes. His explanation of evolution forms the basis for our understanding of the history of life. Darwin was criticized by religious leaders who believed that his ideas were against God.

Reconstruction

Sometimes a lucky find will be a complete skeleton. One example of this is "Lucy," the fossilised remains of an early human ancestor called *Australopithecus*, found in Ethiopia in 1973. The form of the pelvic bone showed the remains to be female, and the formation of the teeth suggested she was about 20 years old. Only 40% of Lucy's bones were found, but because skeletons are symmetrical we know what the missing bones look like.

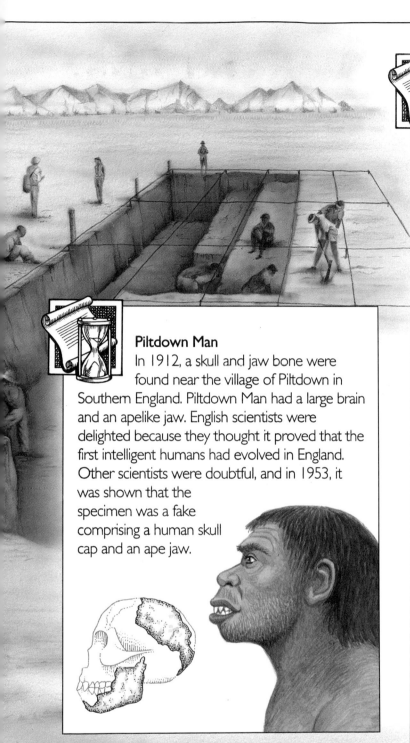

Piltdown Man

In 1912, a skull and jaw bone were found near the village of Piltdown in Southern England. Piltdown Man had a large brain and an apelike jaw. English scientists were delighted because they thought it proved that the first intelligent humans had evolved in England. Other scientists were doubtful, and in 1953, it was shown that the specimen was a fake comprising a human skull cap and an ape jaw.

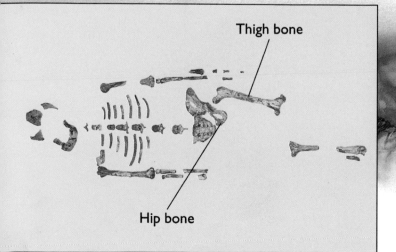

Thigh bone

Hip bone

Famous discoveries

The most important discoveries of early humans have been made in the past 100 years. By 1900, only a few skulls and skeletons had come to light, but many stone tools and pieces of art had been found. During the twentieth century the pace of discovery has quickened, and our understanding of human origins has improved immensely.

Eugène Dubois (1858-1941) found the remains of Java Man, a form of *Homo erectus*, in 1891, the first significant early human fossil. The specimens provoked such fierce debate that Dubois later claimed the bones came from a giant gibbon.

Raymond Dart (1893-1990) was the first to suggest that the earliest human ancestors came from Africa. Here he discovered one of the most important human fossils, the skull of an *Australopithecus*. At first many scientists did not believe that the fossil was human.

Richard Leakey (1944-) has found many human fossils in Africa, notably part of a skull of the oldest known *Homo habilis* fossil dating back 1.9 million years. He also discovered a 1.6 million year old *Homo erectus* skull.

Donald Johanson (1947-) found a series of human fossils in Ethiopia, including Lucy (see left), and he gave *Australopithecus afarensis* its name. He has argued that the first humans could walk upright, but that they had ape sized brains.

OUR FIRST ANCESTORS

Many scientists believe that the separate evolution of apes and humans began between 6 and 10 million years ago. The oldest discovered fossils of our human ancestors are just over 4 million years old. The fossils show that the first humans did not have large brains (see page 5) but they did walk upright. Some scientists believe there were several species living at the same time (see pages 12-13) which is extraordinary to imagine when today there is only a single human species on the Earth.

Geography and human origins

Twenty million years ago, the ancestors of modern apes lived all over Africa. The opening up of the Great Rift Valley, that stretches along East Africa (shaded area below), caused a change in climate. The rain forests shrank, leaving deserts and dry plains. The apes left on the plains stood upright so they could see and move quickly. These apes were our ancestors. The oldest human fossils have been found in the Great Rift Valley area.

Africa

Great Rift Valley area

East African Plains

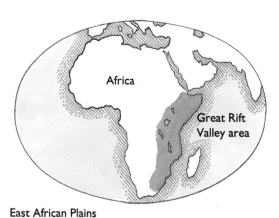

The first human ancestors, species of *Australopithecus*, stood upright. This freed their hands for gathering food, such as these tasty berries from a low tree.

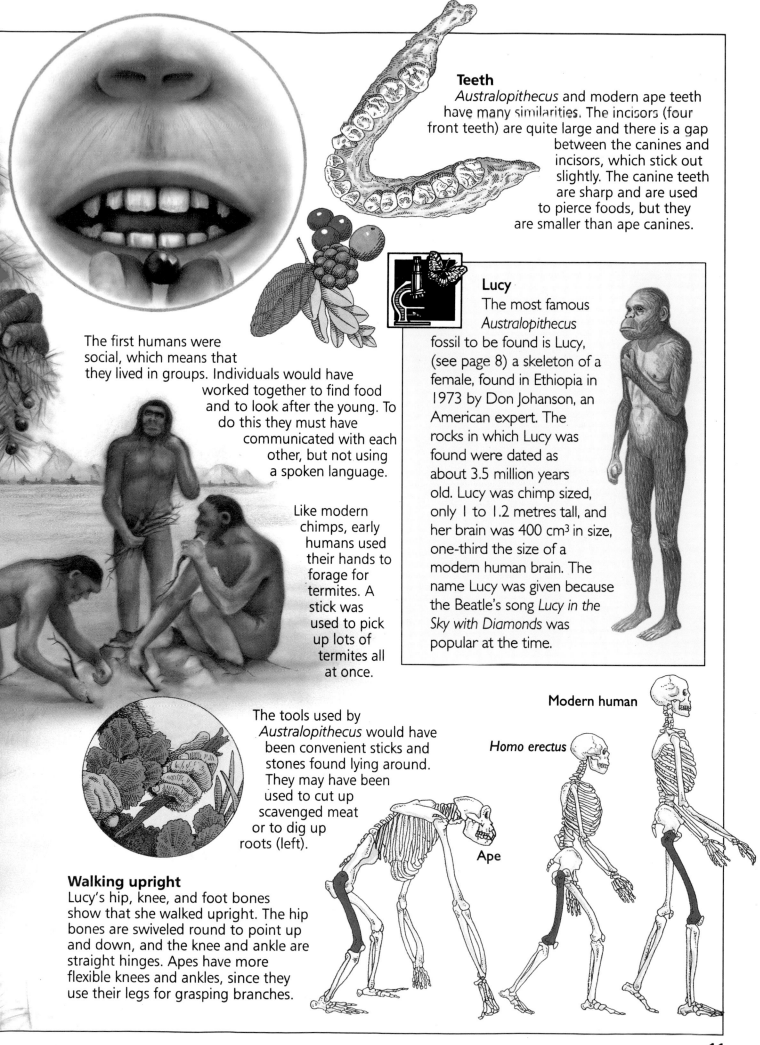

Teeth

Australopithecus and modern ape teeth have many similarities. The incisors (four front teeth) are quite large and there is a gap between the canines and incisors, which stick out slightly. The canine teeth are sharp and are used to pierce foods, but they are smaller than ape canines.

The first humans were social, which means that they lived in groups. Individuals would have worked together to find food and to look after the young. To do this they must have communicated with each other, but not using a spoken language.

Like modern chimps, early humans used their hands to forage for termites. A stick was used to pick up lots of termites all at once.

Lucy

The most famous *Australopithecus* fossil to be found is Lucy, (see page 8) a skeleton of a female, found in Ethiopia in 1973 by Don Johanson, an American expert. The rocks in which Lucy was found were dated as about 3.5 million years old. Lucy was chimp sized, only 1 to 1.2 metres tall, and her brain was 400 cm^3 in size, one-third the size of a modern human brain. The name Lucy was given because the Beatle's song *Lucy in the Sky with Diamonds* was popular at the time.

The tools used by *Australopithecus* would have been convenient sticks and stones found lying around. They may have been used to cut up scavenged meat or to dig up roots (left).

Modern human

Homo erectus

Ape

Walking upright

Lucy's hip, knee, and foot bones show that she walked upright. The hip bones are swiveled round to point up and down, and the knee and ankle are straight hinges. Apes have more flexible knees and ankles, since they use their legs for grasping branches.

THE FIRST HUMANS

It is very difficult to identify a single line of development from *Australopithecus* to the first true humans called *Homo*. Fossil finds in Kenya show that *Australopithecus*, *Homo habilis* and *Homo erectus* were all alive 1.5 million years ago. *Homo habilis*, who evolved around 2 million years ago, was the first to make tools. *Homo erectus*, who evolved around 1.5 million years ago, cooked food on fires and hunted large animals. Such hunting would have required detailed planning and effective communication within the group.

Out of Africa

Homo erectus was the first human to move out of Africa. About 1 million years ago, they moved into North Africa, and across the Middle East to Asia, and later to Europe.

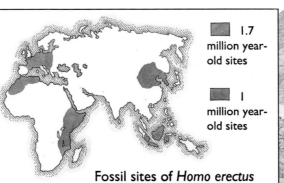

| | 1.7 million year-old sites |
| | 1 million year-old sites |

Fossil sites of *Homo erectus*

Homo erectus foraged for leaves, roots, and fruits as well as hunting for meat. The relationship between *habilis* and *erectus* is not clear, though it is thought that the first gave rise to the second.

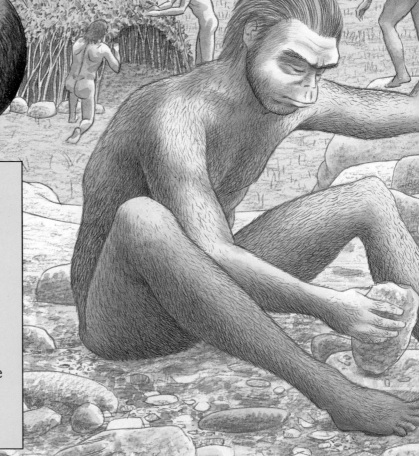

Illness and health

Early humans lived dangerous and exposed lives. They did not have clothing or proper shelters to protect them from extreme heat or cold, and they suffered from many diseases. Some diseases, such as arthritis and tuberculosis damage the bones, and so have been detected in fossils. Food was often scarce, and this must have caused illness too. In many societies today, people commonly live for more than eighty years, but early humans were lucky to reach the age of forty.

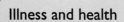

Homo habilis

Homo erectus

Habilis and erectus

Homo habilis ("handy man") evolved 2 to 1.5 million years ago, and *Homo erectus* ("upright man") evolved 1.5 to 0.5 million years ago. *Homo habilis* had a rounded head, flat nose and projecting jaws. *Homo erectus* had a bigger brain and body than *habilis*, and an extremely thick skull.

A family of *Homo erectus* (left) make a fire to cook meat and keep away predators. One of the men is making some stone tools, perhaps to help cut the meat. Evidence of fires was first found in excavations of Peking Man, a Chinese *Homo erectus* who lived 1 million years ago.

Hunter or scavenger

There is no doubt that *Homo habilis* ate meat, but scientists are still not certain whether they hunted large animals actively or whether they scavenged animals. They may have let a larger predator do the killing and then moved in to claim the meat. A site in Africa shows that *erectus* humans took the carcasses of the animals they hunted to their home base and cut the meat off with stone tools. This is shown by the cut markings that have been found on fossilized animal bones.

Sabre-toothed tiger with its prey

Three skeletons

During the 1970s and 1980s Richard Leakey discovered skulls of *Homo habilis, Homo erectus* and *Australopithecus* (left), all dating from the same era. The finds proved that all three species were alive around 1.5 million years ago, putting an end to the idea that humans, unlike any other mammal, had evolved without any variation in species.

MODERN HUMANS

Modern humans all belong to the species *Homo sapiens*. It is thought this species evolved in Africa about 200,000 years ago. Between 100,000 and 35,000 years ago, Europe was home to the Neanderthals, whose brain was the same size as *Homo sapiens* and who some scientists believe were a sub-species of *Homo sapiens*. The Neanderthals were gradually replaced by the Cro-Magnon peoples, *Homo sapiens* who migrated to Europe from the Middle East.

Neanderthals
Neanderthals were strongly built people, who hunted woolly mammoths and rhinos. They made advanced tools and weapons with flint and bone. The Neanderthals disappeared when the ice sheets withdrew from Europe.

Body types
Modern humans show a great range of body sizes and shapes which are suited to the terrain and climate in which they live. Neanderthals, who lived during the Ice Age were short but strongly built, and with much body fat, so they could withstand the cold. Today, modern Inuit (Eskimos) are also short and stocky because they live in the cold. Cro-Magnon peoples were taller, but not as tall as some Modern African peoples, such as the Masai.

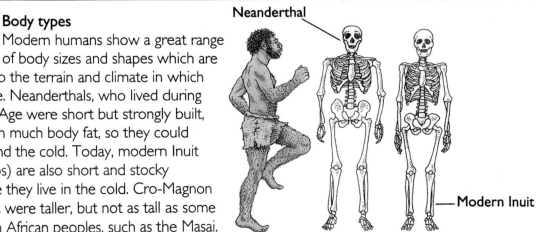

Neanderthal

Modern Inuit

Rafts

Neanderthals and Cro-Magnons made rafts by strapping together logs with thongs made from animal hides. With these simple boats they were able to fish from the middle of lakes or rivers.

Cro-Magnons

The Cro-Magnon peoples lived between 35,000 and 8,000 years ago. The name comes from the Cro-Magnon cave in France where the first skeletons of Cro-Magnons were found. They produced delicate carvings and paintings and made clothes from animal hides, evidence of which have been discovered on dig sites.

Cave art

The Cro-Magnons left beautiful paintings in caves in France and Spain. Many of the images are of animals and sometimes people. The paintings, which date from 20,000 to 10,000 years ago, show that their makers had high artistic skills and exceptional powers of observation.

Cro-Magnon

Modern Masai

MOVEMENT

The australopithecines and *Homo habilis* stayed in Africa but *Homo erectus* and modern man, *Homo sapiens*, migrated to other parts of the world. *Homo erectus* probably spread into Asia and Europe for two reasons: climatic changes and better tools which enabled them to live in a variety of conditions. *Homo sapiens* probably left Africa because of a gradual increase in population. This motivated people to search for new territories in which to hunt and gather food.

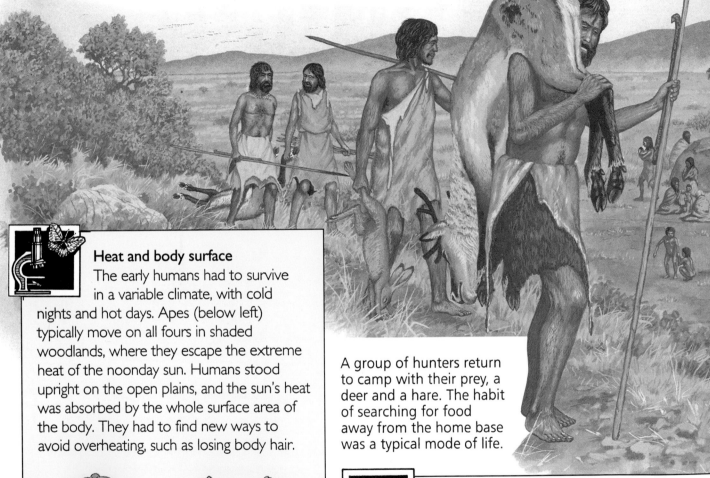

A group of hunters return to camp with their prey, a deer and a hare. The habit of searching for food away from the home base was a typical mode of life.

Heat and body surface
The early humans had to survive in a variable climate, with cold nights and hot days. Apes (below left) typically move on all fours in shaded woodlands, where they escape the extreme heat of the noonday sun. Humans stood upright on the open plains, and the sun's heat was absorbed by the whole surface area of the body. They had to find new ways to avoid overheating, such as losing body hair.

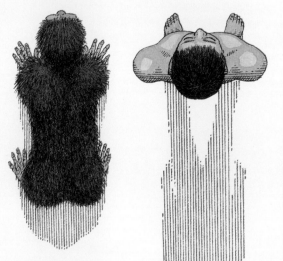

Geographical spread
By gathering evidence from many dig sites around the world, scientists have been able to map the spread of *Homo sapiens* across the Earth. This is shown on the map (right). It is believed that *Homo sapiens* evolved in Africa and migrated into the Middle East and Europe by 100,000 years ago, Asia and Australia by 35,000 years ago, and the Americas by 11,000 years ago.

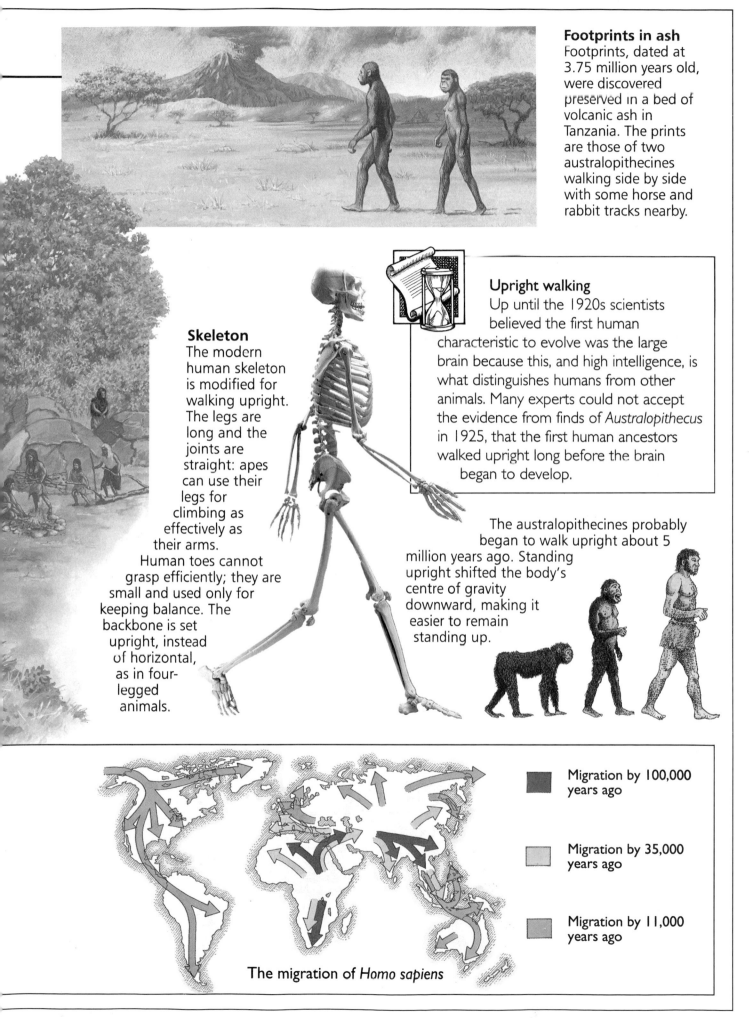

Footprints in ash
Footprints, dated at 3.75 million years old, were discovered preserved in a bed of volcanic ash in Tanzania. The prints are those of two australopithecines walking side by side with some horse and rabbit tracks nearby.

Skeleton
The modern human skeleton is modified for walking upright. The legs are long and the joints are straight: apes can use their legs for climbing as effectively as their arms.
Human toes cannot grasp efficiently; they are small and used only for keeping balance. The backbone is set upright, instead of horizontal, as in four-legged animals.

Upright walking
Up until the 1920s scientists believed the first human characteristic to evolve was the large brain because this, and high intelligence, is what distinguishes humans from other animals. Many experts could not accept the evidence from finds of *Australopithecus* in 1925, that the first human ancestors walked upright long before the brain began to develop.

The australopithecines probably began to walk upright about 5 million years ago. Standing upright shifted the body's centre of gravity downward, making it easier to remain standing up.

Migration by 100,000 years ago

Migration by 35,000 years ago

Migration by 11,000 years ago

The migration of *Homo sapiens*

FOOD

The australopithecines had a mainly vegetarian diet, but later humans ate increasing amounts of meat (see pages 12-13). The availability of certain foods would have been closely linked to the seasons, since there were no means of preserving foodstuffs. Evidence of what early humans ate comes from their tooth formation and from camp sites, where archaeologists have identified seeds, leaves, and bones. 15,000 year old Cro-Magnon cave paintings give some idea of hunting methods.

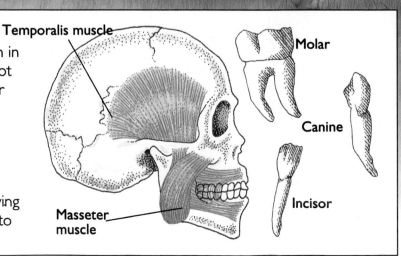

Paintings of hunting
Information about the Cro-Magnons' hunting methods have come from the French and Spanish cave paintings (see pages 14-15). These show people using spears, bows and arrows to hunt now extinct animals such as wild cattle, giant bison and woolly mammoths.

Jaws and teeth
The size and shape of teeth in fossil humans can tell us a lot about diet. By examining teeth under the microscope, scientists have detected scratches and wear marks which indicate the kinds of food early people ate. Modern humans have strong masseter (jaw) muscles that are capable of tearing and chewing tough meat and thick tooth enamel to cope with tough plants and roots.

Temporalis muscle

Molar

Canine

Incisor

Masseter muscle

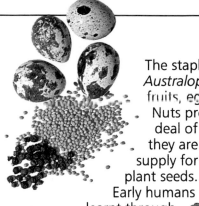

Cooking

Homo erectus probably cooked meat by holding pieces over a fire. Cro-Magnon people wrapped the meat in a leather parcel (below right) and put this into a pot of water which was heated by dropping in red-hot stones.

The staple diet of *Australopithecus* was fruits, eggs and leaves. Nuts provide a great deal of nutrition because they are the food supply for developing plant seeds. Early humans learnt through experience when fruits appeared, which they could eat, and which were poisonous.

Tools for hunting

About two million years ago, *Homo habilis* began to shape stones to make them into better tools. They chipped rocks against each other to create sharp edges. More sophisticated tools, made by *Homo sapiens*, are found from 200,000 years ago; these include carefully shaped arrow heads, harpoons, bows and arrows. The bolas, a set of stones linked by ropes, was an unusual hunting tool, thrown at the legs of a moving animal to trip it up.

Bolas

Modern cowboys using bolas

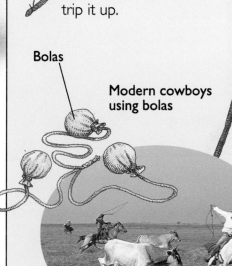

Hunting

Early people caught their prey in a number of ways. The more sophisticated arrows and spears were often used by groups of hunters to kill large animals which would provide a great deal of meat with one kill. The group shown above has used a bolas to bring down a woolly rhinoceros. The animal has then been finished off with spears. The hunters have begun to strip off the meat which will provide a great feast for their group.

HOMES

The australopithecines did not have homes. They wandered in search of food, and would settle for the night in the nearest sheltered spot. The first homes were probably caves and there is evidence that *Homo erectus* built shelters from wood and leaves. Later humans and Neanderthals built tentlike structures out of wood and animal hides. Permanent houses came only much later, when people settled in villages.

Shelters

Shelters could be built quickly from small trees and leaves. These provided protection for older members of the group and for children. In winter the nights would have been cold, even on the African plains, so shelters were necessary for survival.

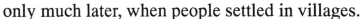

Caves

Evidence found in Europe and China shows that *Homo erectus* lived in caves. Scientists can tell from the build-up of ash, tools and food remains, that some were occupied for many years. Caves make good shelters since they do not require repairs, but they are found only in areas where there are limestone hills.

Clothing

Special stone tools called scrapers have been found on a number of dig sites. These were used for scraping fat from animal hides, and it is likely that the hides were then used for making clothes. Scientists have dated the scrapers at 200,000 years old. Clothing was probably needed only when people moved into the colder climates of Europe.

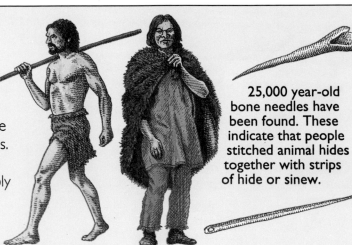

25,000 year-old bone needles have been found. These indicate that people stitched animal hides together with strips of hide or sinew.

Nomadic lifestyle

Most early humans were nomads; they lived by wandering from place to place in search of food. Because of their nomadic existence, Cro-Magnon peoples moved huge distances. Eleven thousand years ago, Alaska was linked to Siberia by a bridge of land and ice (above right). Asiatic peoples were able to cross and settle in the Americas.

Huts in caves

In some places, early people built huts within caves. This gave double protection, especially in cold climates. Huts were built from bent wood covered with animal skins. The huts allowed families to live in larger groups, and also to have their own private shelter.

Mammoth bone huts

The most unusual early huts have been found in Russia. These were built from mammoth bones and animal hides. In the open steppe, there were no stones or trees, and the only large objects were mammoths. Their leg bones and skulls were huge, but one hut required the bones of three or four mammoths.

Animals and early people

Mammoths, woolly rhino and giant bison (right) were common in Europe and North Asia until about 10,000 years ago. They provided early peoples with a source of food and hides. However, these animals quickly became extinct. There are two possible reasons for this: Excessive hunting and climatic changes which led to the rapid spread of forests. Mammoths, rhino and bison were unable to adapt to these environmental changes.

Mammoth

Giant bison

Woolly rhino

TOOLS

The first tool making human was *Homo habilis* (see page 12-13). They made simple tools out of stone, bone, and wood. As humans developed, tool making became more and more sophisticated. Neanderthal and Cro-Magnon peoples made delicate bone needles (see page 20), bows and arrows, and axes. Tools are often the first evidence to be found when scientists begin excavating a site that may have been inhabited by early people.

Hands

Chimps and gorillas have long hands adapted to knuckle walking and for grasping branches. They cannot grip things between their thumb and fingers, as humans can. The human hand is shorter with a flexible thumb long enough to meet the fingers.

Humans can carry out very delicate movements with their hands, like grasping a pencil for writing and drawing.

Apes can grasp sticks, but they cannot perform very precise movements.

Weapons

The selection of tools (above) show the skill of manufacture. They date from the Late Stone Age (Upper Palaeolithic period, 40,000-10,000 years ago). Arrows and harpoons were made by shaping delicate points from stone or bone, and fixing them to straight wooden shafts. Bows required careful stringing of a flexible piece of wood.

Sewing

One of the most specialized tasks in Late Stone Age times was sewing. Bone needles were threaded with sinews or hide strips, and pieces of animal hide were sewn together to make garments and tent covers.

Cutting

Most Palaeolithic tools, such as axes, blades, and scrapers, were used for butchering animals; cutting the meat, cracking the bones, and cleaning the hides.

Flint making

Flint tools were once thought to have been made by people who lived before the Biblical flood. In the 1800s, archaeologists recognized that there was a sequence of tool "cultures", beginning with simple flints and ending with complex tools. The precise order of cultures and accurate dates have only been worked out in the past fifty years.

Weaving

Later Stone Age peoples learned to weave nets from plant fibres, or from thin strips of animal hide. The nets were used for fishing.

Digging

Special digging tools were made, usually from wood (below). These were used to dig up nutritious roots.

Straightening

Special tools made from bone with a hole at one end (above) were used to straighten and smooth sticks to the required shape so they could be used as spear or arrow shafts.

Fire making

To begin with, early humans probably used fire caused by natural forces such as lightning or volcanic eruption. *Homo erectus* probably discovered how to make fire by striking two rocks together to produce a spark. Later peoples discovered more reliable ways to make fire such as the fire drill shown (below).

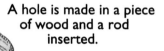

A hole is made in a piece of wood and a rod inserted.

The rod is attached to a bone and leather bow.

The bow is moved rapidly back and forth, turning the rod.

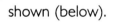

The rod is held in place with a wooden mouthpiece as it turns. The base hole heats up, and and begins to smoulder. Kindling is added and catches fire.

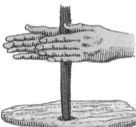

DEATH AND BURIAL

The australopithecines probably did not bury their dead, but later humans had burial ceremonies. Some archaeological sites show that the dead person was carefully laid out before burial, and sometimes provided with food and other objects which were probably meant for use in the after-life. The oldest evidence of this is a 100,000 year old grave of a *Homo sapiens* child found in Israel, whose body had been buried with a deer skull.

Recognizing a burial

Many ancient human remains have been buried by natural processes in layers of sediment. If the body has been deliberately buried, there is clear evidence that the layers of sediment have been disturbed and signs that the hole has been filled in from above.

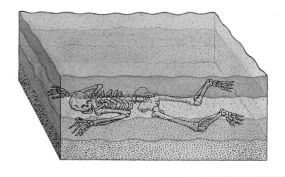

Early music

The oldest musical instruments, flutes and whistles made from bird bones and deer antlers have been found in graves. These date back 30,000 years, and were made by Cro-Magnon peoples. Bird bones make good whistles because they are hollow.

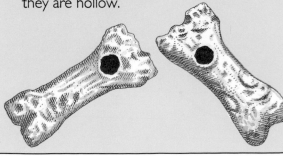

Burial

Here, a group of Cro-Magnons gather round an old man who has just died. The body has been arranged with arms and legs tucked up in what is known as the fetal position, and it is being prepared for burial. One of the men is sprinkling flowers over the body, and another is coating the skin with red ochre (a red pigment found in some soils). These activities are part of a burial ritual, which is watched by the family and friends of the dead man.

Medicine

Most early peoples did not have very effective forms of medicine, which is one reason why so few lived into old age. Remedies would have been passed from generation to generation, such as a knowledge of which plants cured different ailments, and which acted as pain killers. In some early cultures, circles of bone were cut out of the skull of the living patient in an attempt to cure pain.

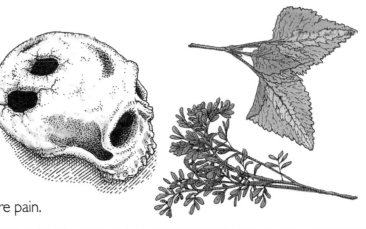

Ritual

It is very difficult to know when humans first began to use rituals, or religious practices. The picture (left) shows a skeleton found buried in the fetal position. Some scientists have suggested that *Homo erectus* used ritualized cannibalism, the eating of human flesh. We know from studying graves that Cro-Magnons used rituals (right) at the time of death. Experts think they believed in a form of life after death, because food was sometimes placed beside the body.

Grave goods

Objects found in graves provide information about ancient religious beliefs. Traces of flowers, such as seeds and pollen, have been found; evidence perhaps that the dead were covered with garlands of flowers. Other items include shells and deer heads, perhaps to ensure successful hunting in the after life. Red ochre stains have been found on bones, so perhaps ritual designs were painted on the dead bodies.

SOCIAL GROUPINGS

Monkeys and apes live in family groups, and so did australopithecines. As humans evolved, groups became more organized; people worked together to build shelters and to hunt (see pages 20-21). Larger cooperative groups would have moved together to find new hunting grounds.

It is from these nomadic groups of people that modern tribes eventually developed.

Childhood
The childhood of early peoples was shorter than it is for modern humans: australopithecines were probably grown up by the time they were ten years old. The children of early humans had a lot to learn. They had to find out how to communicate with older members of the group, how to find food, which berries and nuts they could eat, how to hunt small animals, how to keep warm at night, and so on. Early human babies were probably helpless for the first year or so, just like modern babies, and they had to be carried everywhere.

Babies of *Homo erectus* had to learn how to walk, probably by the time they were one or two years old. By then they would have to be able to travel long distances on foot.

Playing with stones and sticks was a way to learn how to make simple tools. Here a child experiments with two stones.

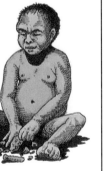

The Flintstones
The most popular cave men are the Flintstones. The Flintstones have featured in dozens of cartoons and in a Hollywood movie. The Flintstones' way of life bears little resemblance to real life in the Stone Age!

Division of labor

It is impossible to tell how early human social groups worked. It is likely that each person had a different job. Probably, like modern nomadic peoples, the women remained close to the home base to look after the children and prepare food. The men would have gone hunting, possibly leaving camp for several days, and returning with meat.

A Cro-Magnon family group go about their daily tasks outside their hide shelters. One man lights a fire using a fire drill (see page 23) while another makes tools. One of the women takes an animal skin into a shelter, and the other looks after a newborn baby.

Domestication

People probably began to raise herds of certain types of tame and useful animals about 9,000 years ago. These animals provided a steady food supply. Dogs may have helped early people by protecting them from danger and helping with hunting.

Language

Most animals have systems of communication to tell each other what they want. Monkeys and apes have complex languages which use sounds, facial expressions, and hand movements. The first humans probably communicated to each other in these ways. Spoken language evolved much later.

Broca's **area of the brain (right) controls the muscles of the mouth and throat that are used in talking.**

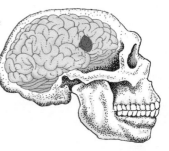

The modern human voice box (left), at the front of the neck, controls the flow of air in and out of the lungs, and allows humans to make complex sounds in speech. The shape of the voice box can be worked out from fossils. Australopithecines had ape-like voice boxes which could not be used for speech.

Facial expressions are very important to us: think of how much easier it is to understand someone you can see talking to you compared to listening on the telephone. Happy and sad faces are easy to tell apart, and there are dozens of other ways in which we can mold our faces.

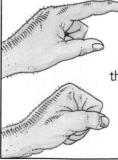

Hand gestures are also important in human communication. Humans use their hands to stress what they are saying, and to point. Early people may have used their hands much more if their voice boxes were less advanced.

THE WAY FORWARD

Much of our understanding of early humans has come in the past ten or twenty years of study. Advances in the field of genetics and more accurate carbon dating methods have provided a great deal of valuable information and there have been some exciting new finds in Africa. However, there are still large gaps in our knowledge; the oldest human ancestors have yet to be found and there are many unanswered questions about how early people lived and behaved towards each other.

Where did the Neanderthals go?

The Neanderthal peoples lived in Europe during the Ice Age. They were a heavier build than *Homo sapiens* but their brains were the same size. They made tools and buried their dead. They died out 32,000 years ago; scientists are not certain why. They may have been killed off by the Cro-Magnons or they could have interbred with them.

Origins of modern humans

There are two quite different views about the origins of modern humans. One is that *Homo sapiens* first evolved in Africa about 200,000 years ago and gradually migrated to Asia, Europe, Australia and the Americas (see page 12). However, some scientists argue that each modern human race evolved separately from populations of *Homo erectus* who began migrating from Africa more than a million years earlier. Complex movements of population led to interbreeding between these separate population groups and allowed *Homo sapiens* to evolve in several places at once.

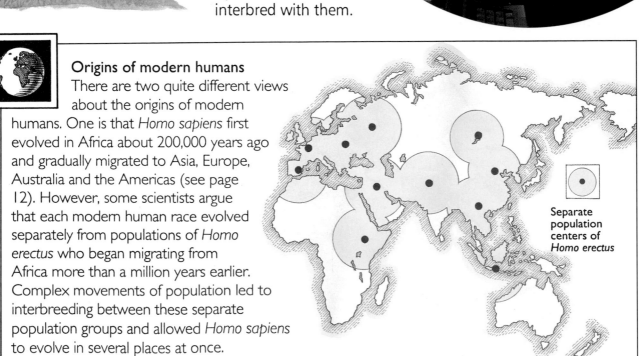

Separate population centers of *Homo erectus*

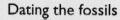

Dating the fossils

Until recently, it was not possible to find exact age dates for older human fossils. Radiometric dating, which measures changes in the amount of chemical decay of natural radioactive elements in the rocks, can give accurate ages. New tests have shown that some early estimates of ages were quite wrong. The skull of Java Man, *Homo erectus*, may be 500,000 years old, but a leg bone, said to come from the same site, may be older.

New technology

When a plant or animal dies radio carbon contained in the tissues decays very slowly. Scientists use a mass spectrometer (far left) to analyze how much radio carbon is contained in a fragment of bone. A piece of bone is burnt and the amount of radio carbon contained in the carbon dioxide given off in the burning process is measured. This is then converted into earth years to give a fairly accurate age of the artifact.

The new find

In August 1994 scientists discovered the oldest remains of our ancestors in Ethiopia. Seventeen specimens of skull fragments, teeth and arm bones have been dated at 4.4 million years old – 500,000 years older than *Australopithecus afarensis*. The finds show that the evolutionary lines leading to humans and apes had split only 4 to 7 million years ago. The shapes of the teeth and elbow show that this species is a human ancestor and not an ape.

Molecular studies

Studing the proteins of animals can give a measure of how closely related they are. Each protein, including DNA, the material in the cell nucleus which records genetic information, evolves at a predictable rate. This means that closely related animals have similar proteins and DNA, and distantly related animals have very different proteins. Molecular studies show that chimps and humans separated about 6 million years ago, and that modern human races separated about 200,000 years ago. Work of this kind is new, and much more needs to be done.

A scientist observes a gorilla in the wild.

IMPORTANT DISCOVERIES

Before 1800
Flint tools were found in gravel beds and caves in many countries. They were thought to be the work of early peoples, but no-one knew quite what they looked like.

1856
Workmen found a complete skeleton in the Neander valley, in Germany, so it was named Neanderthal Man. Some people thought this was a primitive 'cave man', others thought it was a Russian soldier who had got lost.

1865
The first discovery of Stone Age art, a carving of a mammoth in bone, was found in France. This proved, for the first time, that humans had lived side by side with an extinct animal.

1868
The remains of Cro-Magnon peoples were found in France by L. Lartet. The remains were of modern-looking people, and they proved the long history of humans. These were also seen as the makers of the advanced kinds of stone tools that had been found before.

1879
Stone Age cave paintings were found in Spain. These showed that early peoples had had a keen artistic sense, as well as religious beliefs. They also showed aspects of clothing and hunting.

1891
The discovery of Java Man, a form of *Homo erectus* by Eugène Dubois. This was regarded as the missing link, a kind of ape-man.

1912
The hoax of the century. Piltdown Man was found in England, and for a time it was seen as the true human ancestor. In 1953, it was finally shown to be a fake.

1921
The second famous *Homo erectus* population in China, Peking Man, was found. Many specimens came to light, and they were found with remnants of fire and tools.

1924
The skull of a baby from Taungs, South Africa, was announced as the first australopithecine fossil. This was a true missing link, a human being which walked upright, but had an ape brain.

1959
The discovery of *Homo habilis* in the Olduvai Gorge of Tanzania by Louis Leakey. This is the oldest species of *Homo*, and Leakey found evidence that these peoples used very simple tools, the oldest tool-use in the world.

1963
The first studies of human and ape molecules showed that humans and chimps had shared an ancestor only 5 million years ago. This was not accepted at first, since the fossils seemed to show a separate history of 20 million years. The molecular evidence has turned out to be correct.

1974
The most recent famous discovery, Lucy, a small woman of the species *Australopithecus afarensis* was found by Don Johanson in Ethiopia. This is the oldest human species known.

1984
A remarkable nearly complete skeleton of a *Homo erectus* boy was found by Richard Leakey at West Turkana in Kenya. This is one of the most complete specimens of an early human.

GLOSSARY

Ape A primate with a broad chest, no tail and a large brain. Gibbons, orangutans, gorillas and chimpanzees are all apes.

Archaeologist A person who studies ancient remains and artifacts.

Artifact Something made by a person long ago, such as a tool or work of art.

Canine teeth The four long, sharp teeth found either side of the incisors.

Carcass The body of a dead animal.

Carnivore An animal that eats meat.

Communication Passing on or exchanging information from one animal to another, usually by some form of language, using speech, sounds or signs.

Culture The art, language, artifacts and ideas shared by one group of people.

Evolution A gradual change in the characteristics of a population of animals or plants over successive generations. All plants and animals are related back to a single common ancestor.

Fossil The remains of a plant or animal that once lived. Fossils are usually found buried in rock.

Human A large brained primate that walks upright on two legs.

Ice Age A period of time during which a large part of the Earth's surface was covered with ice.

Incisors The chisel-edged teeth at the front of the mouth. Humans have four in each jaw.

Mammal A warm-blooded animal that has a backbone and feeds its young with milk.

Molars The broad grinding teeth situated toward the back of the mouth. Adult humans have twelve molars.

Monkey A primate with a narrow chest, a tail (usually), and which generally lives in trees.

Nocturnal Feeding and moving about at night.

Nomad A wandering person, who moves from place to place.

Omnivore An animal which eats plants and meat.

Palaeolithic (Stone Age). A period of time when early people manufactured their tools from stone. The period began about 2 million years ago and ended about 12,000 years ago.

Palaeontologist A person who studies fossils.

Predator Any carnivorous animal.

Primate A monkey, ape or human, member of the group of mammals that has a large brain, good eyesight and flexible hands.

Scavenging Eating meat from an animal carcass that has been killed by another animal.

Skeleton The bony framework which acts as a support for the body, and to which the muscles are attached.

Species A group of plants or animals that normally interbreed successfully. All members of a species look similar.

Vegetarian A plant eater.

INDEX

Photographic credits
Abbreviations: t-top, m-middle, b-bottom, r-right, l-left.
Front cover t, 9b, 13b, 17, 23tm & tr, 28 all & 29tr - Science Photo Library. Front cover bl, 10 & 23tl - Bruce Coleman Ltd. Front cover br, 16t, 18t, 19t & m - Roger Vlitos. 4 - MGM (Courtesy Kobal). 6bl & 29br - Ardea. 7br, 18m, 26b, 29ml & mr - Frank Spooner Pictures. 8 - Hulton Deutsch. 15b - Mary Evans Picture Library. 19b - Spectrum Colour Library. 24t - Ancient Art & Architecture Collection. 29bl Hulton/ Reuters.